The Gathering Song

poems by

Christina Xiong

Finishing Line Press
Georgetown, Kentucky

The Gathering Song

*For my daughter, Bridget, and for my nieces
Abby, Shelby, Yasmein, Katie, Ava, and Angelina.
You all reside in my heart and in my words, always.*

Copyright © 2018 by Christina Xiong
ISBN 978-1-63534-595-7 First Edition
All rights reserved under International and Pan-American Copyright Conventions.
No part of this book may be reproduced in any manner whatsoever without written permission from the publisher, except in the case of brief quotations embodied in critical articles and reviews.

ACKNOWLEDGMENTS

"Sorting Season" first appeared in *Wild Goose Poetry Review*'s Spring, 2017 issue.

I would like to thank my husband, Dao, for his unflagging support as I composed these poems.

Countless writers have inspired me over the years. I would like to extend a special thanks to my professors and peers at Southern New Hampshire University, especially David Blair.
I am grateful for my professors from the Literature and Language department at The University of North Carolina, Asheville, who helped me grow as an undergraduate writer, especially Richard Chess, a truly exceptional poet and human being.
I owe a debt of gratitude to my dear friend, Meta Commerse, for helping me retrieve the lost parts of my story.

Thank you to the talented photographer Sheila Bogart for providing the stunning photograph for the book's cover.
Thank you to my brother-in-law Tou Vang Xiong for taking my author photos.

Publisher: Leah Maines
Editor: Christen Kincaid
Cover Art: Sheila Bogart
Author Photo: Tou Vang Xiong
Cover Design: Elizabeth Maines McCleavy

Printed in the USA on acid-free paper.
Order online: www.finishinglinepress.com
also available on amazon.com

Author inquiries and mail orders:
Finishing Line Press
P. O. Box 1626
Georgetown, Kentucky 40324
U. S. A.

Table of Contents

Descanso for the Reborn 1

Rootless 3

Transplant 5

Tommy and Stupid Girl 6

Letter to a Former Tenant of my Flesh 8

An Intermittent Habit 10

Labor and Division 13

Doris 17

Grief in Absentia 18

Sorting Season 20

The Singing Hour 21

Clean 22

The Ritual 23

Restoration 24

Rendezvous 26

Stalemate 28

Nagging 29

Potpourri 31

Washing Dishes 32

Descanso for the Reborn

A young man on a motorcycle died
last week on The Devil's Whip.
I didn't know him but I cried
for his family. There should be
a marker for me up there too,
a *descanso* by the roadside,
up The Devil's Staircase,
the name I always use for Highway 80.

I lived up seven miles of switchbacks,
past Buck Creek, and the polished
surface of the man-made lake—
Tahoma. A misnomer. A Cherokee curse.

Past the dam, beneath sheer mountain faces,
boulders where black bears took refuge from cars.
Bats hunted in daylight. Once, I saw
the enormous head of a black wildcat.
A painter, I was assured by an old-timer.

My small pink cottage was pressed gently
against the face of a mountain,
like four leaf clovers preserved in journal pages.
Tangled laurel hells and black locust
trees stood guard over the cove.

Wild turkeys foraged for insects
along Little Buck Creek, which sang
a rushing-water chorus
right outside my bedroom window.
I slept with a sound machine after I left.

Every suitor who visited me there said
this is not what I expected.

The neighbors, all kin to one another, asked
*what kind of a woman lives
alone in a place like this?*
The landlord declared *I don't think she's white.*

I lost myself in those five small rooms.
Paperwork piled up. I stopped opening mail.
Constant rains that year left damp pages
coated with a lace of black mold.
Some of the worst and some of the best
components of myself are still there.

Just once I drove past the holler
and sped up to the top of the Devil's Staircase.
I avoided the loaded .38 Super Colt Commander
on my nightstand, my dead father's gun,
the one I had cradled to my jaw
the night before, while the seventeen-year
locusts screamed.

Each time I stood at a crossroads—
stay or leave? Here or nowhere?—
I walked up beyond the cove, hairpin turns,
never making it farther than the white, steepled church
nestled in the blind curve—
the perfect spot to baptize myself
in one of Little Buck's calmer streams.

Maybe that is where I left her?
My former self?
Where laughing ravens settled, watchful,
into freshly budded branches.
In lavender light from stained glass windows.
Smelling earth, tasting metallic water from the well,
feet going numb in the creek,
burning books and papers, shredding paintings,
plucking herself piece by piece from the wilderness.

Rootless

Buffalo, birth to 8:

An antiseptic burn of snow in my nostrils. A house always under repair. Tar paper peeks through beneath fragments of siding, embarrassing as the satin slip drooping below the hem of my mother's best dress. Cardboard boxes of nails are catalogued, like fossils salvaged from construction sites. Sawdust coats kitchen table. Copper fittings, with their penny odor, litter countertops. Ancient apple trees flank a yard framed in forest and fence. Hydrangea, Queen Anne's lace, peppermint chewed then spat out, its summer flavor medicinal.

Coastal Virginia, 9-21:

Wooden piers stinking of damp salt air, afflicted with barnacles, rank with crabs, heartbeat of conch held to your ear, green waters of swamps, lopsided flight of fish-full pelicans. A place
of concrete bridges strung out across bay, river, creek, reservoir, estuary, ocean—like strands of pearls cascading over a woman's clavicle.

Homelessness and the road, 22-23:

A nowhere place. An in-between place. Creaking pines, purple patchwork tent, flooded meadow, motel room ripe with mildew—bought with forty dollars. An all-night truck stop's greasy grilled cheese and pay-shower. I emerge reborn from the back lot, crawl from a diesel rainbow, from one million miles ridden, through a rumbling sea of eighteen wheelers.

Western North Carolina: Mountains to foothills, 23-present:

Fifteen amber October six-P.M.s, trading sap-golden light for swift mountain dark, swollen shadows over broken corn stalks, like handmade grave markers under an extravagant moon.
The creek sang my name each night and whispered yours each morning. Foothills where muted songbirds flash by, blush-rose bluebird belly dips and flits through half-burnt bamboo. A static
television sky, a hungry hawk circles waiting for a lone chicken—easy

pickings. The woods of yellow poplar, red bud, sourwood, sweet gum, red oak. Avoiding black snake, skunk, and brown recluse spider. A land of whispers, leaf on leaf, rife with saplings, studded with dead sycamores wearing lichen and creeping vines of wisteria weeping purple.

Home, now:

Fine tendrils just sunken into dry red earth, charred remnants of accidental brushfire, ashes of my old letters, a garden left to weed. Sixteen seasons beneath one roof. Replacing property from my first marriage with that of my second. A century-old home, partially restored. The laughter of my daughter. The thick packet of paperwork filed away, showing ownership. Staying.

Transplant

Appalachian people don't accept outsiders.
I will never be a from-here,
not if I live here seventy-five years,
not if I'm buried in the red clay.

When people ask where I am from,
I am tempted to reply nowhere
lest I betray my Yankee birthright.

Eight years of Buffalo winters,
melted into fourteen sweltering summers.
Coastal Virginia humidity clung to me, like illness.

Then Tampa, trees heavy with tangerines,
lilting Spanish drifted through the alley,
bittersweet smoke from a Cuban cigar
wafted through the window-fan.
The air was stale, like the wilted bougainvillea
propped onto the blue porch. Crushed magenta.

I fell in love with Asheville
on a September morning.
A gray one,
when mist billowed off green hills,
a quiet rain fell.
Gold just brushed edges of the foliage,
hints of October's imminent burnishing.
Valley farmlands lay stitched together by fences,
like the ancient symmetry of colorful quilts.

This land took a claim on me,
like the promise I made to the earth
of my ancestral home in Eastern Carolina,
burying my body, as a child, in the sifted soil
of my grandfather's tobacco field.

Tommy and Stupid Girl

Tommy: the pale skin and badly-balding pate
of a Gollum. Thick-necked, muscled chest,
with shoulders like a pit bull ready to pounce.
An indentation in his skull from the kiss
of an oak tree at eighty miles per hour.

When he called me *stupid girl*
for the first time, I got into my car to leave.
He snatched my keys from the ignition,
held them hostage in his huge fist.

Pictures of Christ glued to the gray paint
of his bedroom wall, beside a letter he wrote
to his future-self from prison, a two year stint
for assaulting his last girlfriend. Strangulation.
Thick scars across his throat
from self-inflicted wounds. A rock singer,
his song was the cool fires of a 3 a.m. storm.

Heading to Greasy Creek that night: Road Closed.
Orange reflective sign.
Barricade.
A dead possum moldered on the roadside.
My soft internal voice
that still cared about the outcome
said *turn around, stupid girl.*

Tommy's voice engulfed the walls;
crackling percussive rain, guitar licks
festered like blue-green flames
against the doorframe.
He prayed in tongues.

I tried to outrun him,
down the dark gravel road.
There were no bars on my phone.

No signal, and I should have known,
it would have been so much better,
if I had just stayed home.

He brandished a knife, ready to ravage
his forearm, open up his jailhouse tattoo.
My arms flew up. He pulled the strings.
Dance marionette. Dance, *stupid girl.*
Into the dark trailer with its plywood walls.
His hands grasped my throat.

A steaming mug of Tension Tamer tea
tilted in my hand and spilled.
I wondered why I took the detour.
Road Closed.
Aftertaste of chalky pills.
Stupid girl. God was watching out.
I ignored the signs and drove around.

I never told what I had to do to leave.
After that night, I always carried
an extra set of keys in my pocket,
or tucked inside my bra, close to my body.

Nightmares later:
Tommy wrapped around me
pale, alien. Incubus.
A rattle at the screen door,
and my heart raced like the feral dog
who scavenged through my neighborhood,
galloping past with protruding ribs
and bloody froth at the mouth.

Letter to a Former Tenant of my Flesh

Dear Pearl,
Oh, my girl—you had it all—
    didn't you?
        Everything in the world.   The black lace
           bustier, fishnets, that designer satin skirt,
        your sole couture.
All of those long brown curls hanging down
    your back, a candy-pink kissprint on the rim of your glass.

    You had two—no—three—
        maybe four—fingers, or a full fist, of amber
        whiskey to drink, and couldn't pay your tab.
  Rails of coke hit the back of your throat in a diesel-
    flavored burst. You danced—no, more like grabbed—
        dragging needle-sharp canines over men's necks.

You tongued their sweat like a salted glass rim,
            never tried to hide your throaty laugh
    before throwing back shots someone sent,
        locking eyes with J. C., your dealer,
  who sent more shots in your honor—no,
        dishonor—because your breast slid
from the bustier, exposing a large, purplish nipple.

You blacked out, again, remembering little.

Oh, Pearl, why did you leave me?
  Your old bar downtown is out of business.
     Your favorite neon sign in the pawnshop window,
       the blue guitar, burned out.
         Your shoulders are much too narrow now.
           Your breasts are too shrunken to fill that lacy bustier.
            Your sober throat can't screech out Janis at karaoke.
              Your eyes don't have the feline glint.

But you left something wild,
    a gem embedded in my eyelid,
        parallel scratches in the mirror,
            the memory of your wet mouth
                leaving me thirsty.

An Intermittent Habit

I went outside to smoke and found a poem.
It's a disgusting habit I just recently picked up
again. The one-eyed oak tree must have taken mercy
on me, then laid this poem at my feet. I have left
offerings at its roots before, field-stripped tobacco.
One of the eyes fell off some time ago. We never found it.

I stood on our land waiting for the call of the barn owl,
the black snake slithering, uninvited.
Waited for that feeling
of relief to come over me. *Sanctuary*,
I exhale the word in menthol smoke.
I need a security camera, or a dozen.
Floodlights, night vision goggles, a large stick.
I need a gate across the drive. Five German shepherds
trained to go for the throat. Fences. Electrical. Barbed wire.

I need for the sound of gravel crunching beneath my shoes
to stop reminding me of my desperate feet
trying to flee from my once-captor,
for the look of certain balding men to stop making my neck
muscles spasm. Remember the way I laughed at you
for locking the windows at night, and drawing the blinds?
We have no neighbors, who are you afraid of?
Remember when I lived alone, with the comfort of a gun?
Remember when I lived alone, still, without steel beneath my pillow?

I need alarms, surveillance, martial arts training.
The oak tree, the maple, and the poplar are tinged
brown. Their leaves mottled with Round-Up drift.
I need a bio-dome to cover these old-growth trees.
I need a respirator, a gas mask, water-cleansing tablets.
I need my freshly-issued permit to purchase a handgun
to translate into a 9mm, ample ammo.
I need an uncanny skill in marksmanship that I have never possessed.
I need cans of beans resistant to radiation.

I need a new language, a code, trustworthy people fluent in speaking it.
I need a mailbox with a padlock, a tiny slot for inserting junk mail.
A post office box, steel shutters for the windows.
I need a safe, a panic room, a bunker.

I do not mind the raven's shrieking, but I mind
wolf-spiders making it into the house.
I do not mind coyotes stealing whole watermelons
from the garden to feed their pups,
or the stray dog meandering across the land,
but a drunk woman named Stephanie pounding on my door
demanding help in the night from a stranger,
my bleeding-heart husband opening the door,
my feeling of doom slipping behind the wheel
to drive her away from my family, that, I mind.
No peace of mind could be spared, no sanctuary given.

The land spirits are exhausted and starving.
Pesticides and herbicides have weakened my guardians.
Wind has half-blinded my battle-scarred oak.
I long for the strong woman who used to sleep in my body.
I long for her assurance that she could pick up the receiver always
on her bedside table and dial 911. Before that time when they came,
annoyed, unwilling to remove the trespasser from the house
where she lived alone, when she hid bruises on her wrists in the shape
of a man's hands. Before she knew of the frequent, unjust, killings.

Before she had anything to lose, only her collection of books,
something of no value to the Stephanies or the rough-handed men
inhabiting every town with their depraved, bottomless needs.
Before the poems she wrote unearthed words that left her quaking
in her skin. Before goosebumps rose on her arms in warm wind.
Before the twenty-first century nightmare she had of being doxxed
made her want to delete her existence out of her laptop.
Before the storm blew through, barely a tropical depression

when it brushed past, but she hoarded bottled water,
flinched at flickering lights and through the weather report.

Maybe I am a broken woman.
Maybe I am the branch that does not bend.
Maybe I am the missing clay eye of the great tree.
Maybe I am the fiery death on the road's shoulder.
Maybe I am the burning woman dropping from the ninetieth story.
Maybe I am Stephanie claiming *I had a seizure back there.*
Maybe I am the woman with the hidden bruises.
Maybe I am the bereaved leaning over her lover's coffin.
Maybe I am the hungry woman roaming in darkness.
Maybe I am the mother carrying her child away from a bombed out city.
Maybe I am the person waiting on the roof as the water rises.
Maybe I am a witness who will never be the same.
Maybe I need a witness, someone to alter forever,
or maybe I should stop smoking, the habit I pick up
when I can't sit with myself anymore,
when I summon each inhalation to bring cancer,
when there is nowhere left for me to go.

Labor and Division

I.

In the early hours, there was a wooden rocking
chair, a red cushion tied to its spindle-back.
I dripped lavender essential oil onto cotton balls,
played Hindi chants on my headphones,
"Universal Mother" was the title track that dipped me into trance.

My husband drew me a warm bath, surprised
the labor and delivery room had a tub.
Clean white porcelain cradled me until water cooled.
I was no longer soothed by weightlessness.
He watched me sink into the hospital bed.

Epidural pressed me down like stacks of lead
vests, the kind you wear for x-rays at the dentist.
He kept watching me, his brown eyes attentive
as a newborn mother memorizing her infant.
Thirty hours had passed, the room still dim,

neither of us slept nor ate. Then fruitless hours
of pushing began. My legs braced against
nurse and husband. Numb from the waist
but feeling my way through the haze
hovering in the room like alcohol fumes.

Soon I was wheeled to the surgical theater.
I could see my breath in unwavering light,
heard the soft cry of my baby daughter
before her father strode across my iceberg to her.
I caught one glimpse of her pointed head,

felt blood pooling on my torso,
as they sewed me back together.

II.

Ten hours after the caesarean delivery
of my daughter, I am rushed back into
surgery. Some taproot artery gushes
into my abdominal cavity. I am glib
as they wheel me away.
In the recovery room I joke with nurses.
I am an anomaly,
barely touched by sedation.

When I return to the maternity ward
nurses pull back the sheet and find
I am floating in my own blood.
Give me Versed, I beg the anesthesiologist
I don't want to remember.

He nods looking scared.
They all look scared.
The amnesia drug slips into my vein,
but the quiet forgetting is later recalled in nightmares.
I am crushed, in slow motion,
like a recurring dream I had in childhood,
my worst one, of being flattened by a boulder.

Motherhood opens something up
that cannot be contained by multiple sutures
and requires two blood transfusions.
I almost didn't sign the release for a transfusion
at my pre-delivery visit, but I made a crack
about not wanting to die, then signed.

Heading to the hospital for my induction
we stop for greasy diner food, *my last meal*
I tell the server who flinches
like I struck him.

Even my husband, never superstitious,
corrects me.

In intensive care
a large seam above my pelvic bone, both divides me
and holds me together.
Wires and machines
anchor me to the bed.

My baby is on another floor of the hospital.
She was born perfect.
Before labor, I bargained with God
that if one of us should suffer
it would have to be me.
Answered prayer.
The narcotics can't ease missing
those first days of her existence.

Nothing softens the doctor's words:
> *If you have more children,*
> *you will die.*

Like my great-grandmother
who hemorrhaged in childbirth at 38,
the age I am now. She and her infant son
went together. I learn I will never
have a son of my own, and something cracks,

right down the middle of me.
I cannot look at the tracks of stitches
across my middle,
clean my wound which weeps,
nurse my infant,
take any food or drink by mouth,
or empty the contents of my stomach
which are drained from a tube in my nose.

The doctor told me widespread numbness would persist
but I would grow used to it.
I have.
I can almost feel my thighs again.

After one year, I can touch my scar
but only in the bathtub.
I smooth lavender oil into its crease.

Almost two years later,
my womb encased in a cage of scar tissue,
a physical therapist says my dissociation
from my lower half is *not normal.*

One day the trauma will be distant, faded
but not forgettable.
My adhesions will respond
to these constant manipulations,
soften their grasp on my organs.

I may find a son borne by someone else
sleeping in my house.
I can finally put myself back together.

Doris

I saw my mother for fifteen minutes
after school, in her uniform of factory blue.

Six p.m. she stumbled out the door.
Drove off, reeking of coffee, cigarettes.
Gone for the duration, nights.

She became part of the factory
a machine's moving part,
component of a grinding beast
no human being could identify.

A ghost, name embroidered across
navy shirt, a cold uneaten supper.

Her body belonged to the factory.
Dresses hung limp in her closet.
Hands swelled and gnarled into twisted roots.

When she could finally put on rings
and eyeliner, it was a struggle.
Her hands were not her hands.

Dresses once brushed
curves of a woman with light
in her, rippling like light on water.

Her hands fried chicken, boiled corn,
planted pansies. A scent of onions and French
perfume clung to auburn hair.

Two a.m. when I woke fevered,
I lowered myself into a single
inch of tepid water to cool delirium.

I waited in dark afternoons,
only person in the silent house,
waited wearing her flowered dresses.

Grief in Absentia

In the year I swore off grief
I lost my favorite uncle, then my last living
grandparent, my paternal grandmother,
Kathleen. I fixate on her
black and white wedding photograph.

Kathleen's dress seems sewn onto her slender frame,
draped elegantly, like fabric covering an unfinished sculpture.
Irish lace made by a flotilla of Irish nuns
floats like a nimbus around her pale form.
Her red hair is dimmed a deep grayish
black in the photograph's limited perception.

We were close when I was small.
Sunday meals at her house, before
my parent's divorce took me
from my birthplace in upstate New York.

My father's funeral with its folded flag
was the first time I had seen her in twenty-five
years. A series of strokes rendered her largely
silent. There was an occasional outburst.

Her tremulous speech, reminded me of her
sudden correspondence in recent years:
A $100 bill sent through the mail,
the congratulatory note written by someone
else—an assisting relative, stranger to me—
or the card in her post-aneurysm scrawl
containing an empty gift certificate sleeve.

She sent boxes of carefully bubble-
wrapped heirloom crystal. Waterford
votive holders, an ancient candy dish.

In January, she died of another stroke.
During the Women's March I lit votive candles
in her candleholders and nursed my daughter
through a childhood illness.
Somehow a mantle of strength
gathered around me—lead crystal,
frothy lace—my grayish-black hair that might have been red,
if I started out with more of my grandmother in me.

Her answers only came through
in her penetrating absence,
latent Irish awakening in my veins,
a steely fortitude
proclaiming
I am you. I am you.

Sorting Season

Preoccupied with thoughts of my own
death, I venture into eaves,
extract the mammoth plastic tote
wedged behind flatware and sewing needles.
The corkscrew stored here half-a-decade meant
sobriety and sacrificing my near-yearly foray
into the mass grave of incomplete suicide
notes, letters from dead relatives, forests
of declarations. Old growth trees strewn with ink;
the woody scent of their pulp familiar as grandma's
house, like talcum powder, musty guest sheets.

Obsolete as photographs from my first
wedding, that pale girl of twenty with a careful
stranger's half-guarded expression.
It's been recommended
I burn the lot. All these skeletons
collapse into ash. Faded penciling in teenaged journals
no one will ever love me what did I know
then of *ever*?
A silent bride in expired
photographs, of her I know nothing.

The Singing Hour

The eastern sky falls blue,
while sunset washes the western window
in baby-pink. Maroon-lined clouds caress
the swell of the green mountain.

In our bedroom, I sing.
The vibrations of my throat gather
my family to the room. Even cat paws
sink into the rug beside me; she curves
into a C at my bare feet.

My husband kneels at the foot of the bed,
head bowed like a supplicant. Sometimes
he snores, sucked into accidental slumber
by the lullaby intended to soothe our infant
daughter. I pull breath deeply from
my diaphragm, feeling her squirm against
my belly. She becomes limp and heavy.
Her eyelashes flutter against her cheeks.

The window glass cools, a streetlight turns on.
Around me, they nestle, sigh
in sleep. The last note finds me
in darkness.

Clean

As a child, cleaning became my religion.
From my mother's side, her Pagan tendency.
Kneeling, I applied lemon-scented Pledge,
glossing the coffee table in prayer.
Vacuuming the carpet, like a penance.
I was reprimanded for wearing down
expensive fibers with my ministrations.

I polished hardwood floors, their waxy buildup
made people slip. I scrubbed doors until paint
came off on my rag. Bathrooms were baptized
in the ammonia burn of Comet powder.

Once a year, my mother would take bric-a-brac
down from her numerous shelves: tea cups, saucers—
none matching—a collection of old tin
canisters filled with loose buttons, trinkets
resting alongside Hummels and German
beer steins saved from her brief time overseas.
Wiped with a rag dipped into a bucket
of sudsy, diluted Murphy's Oil Soap.

Clean smells, a sudden reverent order.
The way she rearranged items, like altars:

even the dried husks of insects, minerals,
feathers, shells, and *milagros* she collected,
scattered haphazardly among knick-knacks,
beside several out of print antique
books on anatomy or poetry.

Even now when seasons change I wash windows.
Each object in the house is blessed with cloths
and chemicals, every windowsill
and baseboard is rubbed free of dirt and grime.
Things I can put my hands on are made new.

The Ritual

When I get the call that another relative has died
I pull out canisters of sugar and flour, measuring
spoons and mixing bowls. I mash overripe bananas
long past mellowing, pour buttermilk into a Pyrex cup,
crack two eggs into a glass bowl and whisk them gently,
a tablespoon of vanilla extract follows.
Within an hour I have a golden fragrant loaf.

I don yellow Rubbermaid gloves, nearly elbow-high,
dilute Clorox into my plastic silver bucket, attack
mold in the grout of tiles with a scrub brush,
erase the tub's ring of soap scum, kill
any remaining germs, polish mirrors with vinegar
then the stainless faucet and porcelain sink.
Within an hour the bathroom is disinfected and sparkles.

I strip sheets from the mattress, replace
them with crisp white Egyptian cotton, my best set.
I put woven blankets into the washer on a gentle cycle,
shake the quilt until dust swirls,
pull out the vacuum, with its hepa filter, assault
carpet, suck cobwebs from ceiling fans and corners.
Within an hour my bed is made with dryer-warm blankets.

I brew strong tea, chai or Constant Comment,
something spiced, light a white seven-day candle, burn white
sage, or copal, draw a bath of scalding water
with sea salts, a few drops of bergamot oil.
Fifteen minute soak, dry off, dress in pajama pants
and t-shirt, eat a slice of banana bread, drink my tea.
Within an hour, I climb into bed cradling a box of Kleenex.

Restoration

Antiquing, my husband crawls beneath roll top desks.
He taps surfaces, determining if wood is genuine,
turns over chairs in search of brand markings.
His black hair is peppered by a fine layer of dust.
When he knocks on a buffet proclaiming *it's veneer,*

it takes me back to our first date:
after lunch we walked to a secondhand furniture shop.
He bought a duck head rocking chair.
Some people say it is a goose neck rocker,
but we still call it a duck head rocker.

One of us made a comment about rocking our babies
as I sat in the tattered floral chair, a statement
which seemed premature even to me, a woman yearning
for motherhood, like a cracked seed waiting for rainfall.
Months later, after we had moved my mountain
of belongings into his mostly-empty bungalow.
He said *you know that's your chair, right?*

He had never upholstered furniture before,
but he is one of those people who is good
at everything he does. He reupholstered it in gold fabric,
glued laced ribbon along its edges.
I rubbed the wood with lemon oil until it gleamed.
My hands cherished the curved feel of the duck head
arms under my cotton cloth.

The day we brought our daughter home,
I nursed her in that rocking chair.
It was one of the few times she suckled effortlessly,
before my milk went dry too soon.
She turned two years old last week,
rarely lets me rock her anymore.

It is hard not to feel sentimental over a gift
like this, cradling the only child we will ever have.
I remember promises we seemed to give
on that first date, one of those seldom truths
we knew before we should have,
of the beautiful things we would make together.

Rendezvous

If it's a fantasy you should
be able to walk into a field of lavender,
find a cool clearing, settle
down on a pillow of buds, velvet confetti.

In a fantasy there is no
stinging mosquito,
no sweat trickling in your eyes,
or squinting from noon's platinum hangover.

Please explain what these baskets of wrinkled laundry,
unfolded factory uniforms,
are doing here, in our daydream?
Or these dishes encrusted with dried egg?
Or these diapers souring in the can?

If you bed down in a fragrant field of ticks and horseflies
you will awaken diseased and bloody
a trace of your lover,
imprinted on wet thighs,
and a mouth tasting of poison.

Even in a fantasy, if the farmer sprays pesticides
over the prickly patch of earth you've burrowed into
you may develop a permanent tinge of cancer.

You cannot imagine the cream of your lover's throat
skimmed by your lips,
pupils dilating like the rising new moon,
or sighs, gasps, rough
exhalations you've been holding.

Even in a fantasy, you don't inhale the lavender blooms' mint
or the tang of moss dewed over.
A hungry baby is crying somewhere in a maze of flowers
demanding to be fed.
Lovers lie back to back, hands tucked beneath their faces.
You study stacks of unpaid bills,
sort grocery lists, pick up blood pressure pills,
clip coupons to tuck away, forget, but never miss.

I remember when you told me my eyes looked
like a star nebula, and I go there in a fantasy,
to that fancy sea of fluorescence.
You're invited, but you're bathing the spaghetti-flecked baby.

Your hands are buried in flour,
            kneading bread,
            painting the house,
            killing hornets,
            changing lightbulbs,
            winterizing windows.

I ask again, but I don't think you hear over the complaining
whir of the leaf blower
pushing dried lavender
blossoms to the edges
of a fallow field I invented.

Stalemate

I can never leave arguments unresolved,
dive into my pillow, shutter my eyes,
welcome the rest of a guileless child.

Instead I sit awake, ignoring
the rending centered in my chest.
I listen to three clocks
tick out asynchronous rhythms.

I have one clock or more in every room.
Each room of my house has its own hollow cadence,
the passage of time measured out in telemetries.

Clocks transcribe messages in audible Morse code:
breathe, be still, exhale through the ball of fire
in my throat, a clot of unshed tears
tinged with chlorine, sanitized tap-water grief.
The clocks' metronome ricochets,
relentless as cicadas mating and dying:

all summer long, they fill the voided night
with plaintive music that stirs me.
Clocks and insects keep vigil with me,
over my stunned silence. Until I retreat
to my side of a shared bed. Curl into
my pillow, invite the salt-release,
my own sweet unfurling, the answering cry.

Nagging

Thirteen months after I told him
the roof is leaking,
and his excuse was:
rain blows sideways,
siding needs replacing,
gutters clog with effluvia, decaying leaves.
I say *we'll see,*
as fresh water stains metastasize,
random Rorschach blots, piss-yellow.

Original pine floors from 1920,
once painstakingly refinished, now buckle.
Ceiling tiles bulge,
rain down finely sifted dust, like flour.
I hope that's not asbestos.
An upstairs cave-in leaves jagged ceiling.
A dehumidifier is bought on credit.
I harangue him monthly,
thankful for drought, until fires come;
a haze of forest-death settles in the valley.

Long prayed-for rains beat down
on the rusted tin roof,
summoning guilt-free quiet
during the baby's nap.
My husband approaches,
says *the roof is leaking.*
One eyebrow leaps,
an exaggerated *grand jeté.*
Oh. Really?

He responds:
It dripped on my foot.
Water leaked through
where a screw came loose.

Thirteen months,
hassling him,
too short to reach the attic myself
and investigate
all the damage
caused by something miniscule.

Potpourri

This disastrous fall
I just want a reprieve,
while ink dries on the cream paper
of my husband's naturalization certificate.

For once, to be the type of woman
I've wished toward
decorating the yard with small bales of hay,
mums, a pumpkin, and a smiling scarecrow
stitched from recycled fabrics.

Instead, I craft a poem stitched together
in pilfered moments, punctuated
by stolen sips of perpetually cold coffee.

I peel an orange for my daughter's breakfast,
a Cara Cara, pink and bland. I strip rinds,
scraping pulp away, like pieces of dead winter-skin
I carve from my thick heels with a razor.

I arrange orange rinds and apple peels
onto a plate, add cinnamon sticks, cloves,
place the concoction into a copper pot
to simmer on the stove.

We will stay indoors on a rainy day
building blanket forts.
Potpourri will soothe the dread that clings to me,
like a toddler's arms wrapped around my neck.

Reminded of low-budget traditions my mother kept up
during my childhood. Making something lovely from nothing
makes me feel resourceful. Even if it is futile,
like untangling the fine silk of my daughter's curls.

Washing Dishes

My mother tells a story about my childhood
love of washing dishes. I'd stand on a kitchen chair,
wobbling where the floor of the century-old house slanted.
Iridescent bubbles of Dawn detergent floated
to the sunlit window overlooking my mother's garden.
My tiny hands fit inside drinking glasses
in a useful way. I always washed the glasses first.

I gathered egg shells and coffee grounds,
after the dishes were draining in the rack,
I took composted scraps into the garden
and spread them beneath my mother's tomato plants.

Now in my own century-old house,
the kitchen window frames our bamboo
grove and my husband's wild garden.
He plants seeds, waits for rain, and brings in
a haphazard harvest: waxy zucchinis, crisp cucumbers,
whatever survives despite insistent weeds and rabbits.

Though the moles grew fat last summer
on "Russian Beauty" sunflower seeds,
there was still an end-of-summer row of stragglers
tilting their beauty-heavy faces upward,
guarding prostrate rows of trampled corn that didn't make it.

I have spent untold hours standing here,
hands in soapy water until they prune,
until they are cracked and raw. Washing
baby bottles while I damned my empty breasts
for the half-curdled daily mess.
Disappointed after family parties
because nobody touched the food.

Side by side with my husband, hips bumping,
as I washed and he rinsed. Weeping into dishwater
when I was grieving my grandmother
and nobody offered condolences.
The dishes always need washing,
I complained on the phone to my mother,
and she would tell that story again
about my childhood love of washing dishes,
but I couldn't remember ever loving such a chore.

When my husband brought our new dishwasher home,
a stainless steel, gleaming rectangle of modernity,
I didn't know whether I should laugh or cry.
I looked out the window at the silent bamboo,
and finally remembered that chair rocking under my feet,
the tilt of the floor, my mother's eyes watching,
and my tiny hands making the glasses sparkle.

Christina Xiong has been searching for home her entire life. She has had three last names and seventeen addresses. Christina holds an MA in English and Creative Writing from Southern New Hampshire University and a BA in Literature and Creative Writing from the University of North Carolina at Asheville. Writing has been her lifeline and her passion since she was a small child. Christina believes in the healing power of language. She is a certified Story Medicine facilitator and a certified North Carolina peer support specialist. She lives in the foothills of Western North Carolina with her husband, daughter, and feline familiar. When she is not writing, reading, or working a path of healing and recovery, she enjoys cooking from scratch and rummaging through antique stores.

www.ingramcontent.com/pod-product-compliance
Lightning Source LLC
LaVergne TN
LVHW041604070426
835507LV00011B/1300